TÜM DÜNYA
TEK MILLET

Greatest Country on
Earth is Earth

ABHIJIT
NASKAR

Fabric of Humanity
Build Bridges not Walls: In the name of Americana
The Constitution of The United Peoples of Earth
Lives to Serve Before I Sleep
When Humans Unite: Making A World Without Borders
All For Acceptance
Monk Meets World
Mission Reality
Citizens of Peace: Beyond The Savagery of Sovereignty
Operation Justice: To Make A Society That Needs No Law
See No Gender
The Gospel of Technology
Every Generation Needs Caretakers: The Gospel of
Patriotism
Aşkanjali: The Sufi Sermon
Mad About Humans: World Maker's Almanac
Revolution Indomable
When Call The People: My World My Responsibility
No Foreigner Only Family
Hurricane Humans: Give me accountability, I'll give you
peace
Ain't Enough to Look Human
Servitude is Sanctitude
Time To End Democracy: The Meritocratic Manifesto
I Vicdansaadet Speaking: No Rest Till The World is Lifted
Boldly Comes Justice: Sentient not Silent
Good Scientist: When Science and Service Combine
Sleepless for Society
Neden Türk: The Gospel of Secularism
Martyr Meets World: To Solve The Hard Problem of
Inhumanity
The Shape of A Human: Our America Their America
When Veins Ignite: Either Integration or Degradation
Heart Force One: Need No Gun to Defend Society
Solo Standing on Guard: Life Before Law
Generation Corazon: Nationalism is Terrorism
Mucize Insan: When The World is Family
Hometown Human: To Live For Soil and Society
Girl Over God: The Novel
Gente Mente Adelante: Prejudice Conquered is World
Conquered
Earthquakin' Egalitarian: I Die Everyday So Your Children
Can Live
Giants in Jeans: 100 Sonnets of United Earth

Vatican Virus: The Forbidden Fiction (Abi Naskar
Adventures Book 2)
Karadeniz Chronicle: The Novel (Abi Naskar Adventures
Book 3)
Şehit Sevda Society: Even in Death I Shall Live
Handcrafted Humanity: 100 Sonnets For A Blunderful
World
Mücadele Muhabbet: Gospel of An Unarmed Soldier
Making Britain Civilized: How to Gain Readmission to The
Human Race
Dervish Advaitam: Gospel of Sacred Feminines and Holy
Fathers
Honor He Wrote: 100 Sonnets For Humans Not Vegetables
The Gentalist: There's No Social Work, Only Family Work
Either Reformist or Terrorist: If You Are Terror I Am Your
Grandfather
Woman Over World: The Novel (Abi Naskar Adventures
Book 4)
High Voltage Habib: Gospel of Undoctrination
Bulldozer on Duty
Find A Cause Outside Yourself: Sermon of Sustainability
Ingan Impossible: Handbook of Hatebusting
Amor Apocalypse: Canım Sana İhtiyacım
Amantes Assemble: 100 Sonnets of Servant Sultans
Mucize Misafir Merhaba: The Peace Testament
Divane Dynamite: Only truth in the cosmos is love
Sin Dios Sí Hay Divinidad: The Pastor Who Never Was
Corazon Calamidad: Obedient to None, Oppressive to None
Esperanza Impossible: 100 Sonnets of Ethics, Engineering &
Existence
Mukemmel Musalman: Kafir Biraz, Peygamber Biraz
Himalayan Sonneteer: 100 Sonnets of Unsubmission
Yarasistan: My Wounds, My Crown
The Centurion Sermon: Mental Por El Mundo
Her Insan Ailem: Everyone is Family, Everywhere is Home
Humankind, My Valentine: World's First Anthology of 1000
Sonnets
Aşk Mafia: Armor of The World
Vande Vasudhaivam: 100 Sonnets for Our Planetary Pueblo
Visvavictor: Kanima Akiyor Kainat
Sapionova: 200 Limericks for Students
Rowdy Scientist: Handbook of Humanitarian Science
Insan Himalayanoğlu: It's Time to Defect

DEDICATION

To the people of one earth.

CONTENTS

1. Vicdansaadet Sonnet

Sonnet 1238

Vicdansaadet, The Sonnet

I have many names,

Sometimes I am Hometown Human,
Sometimes I am Mucize Insan,
Sometimes I am Ingan Impossible,
Sometimes I am Mukemmel Musalman,

Sometimes I am Dervish Advaitam,
Sometimes I am Bulldozer on Duty,
Sometimes I am Corazon Calamidad,
Sometimes I am High Voltage Habib,

Sometimes I am Himalayan Sonneteer,
Sometimes I am The Gentalist,
Sometimes I am Divane Dynamite,
Sometimes I am Rowdy Scientist.

These all look and sound so different,
because you are distant in culture.
Move past the circus of manmade caves,
within every heart you'll find a Naskar.

Call it Naskar, Shams or Adi Shankara,
it is all but one spirit of oneness.
Wherever the fire of integration
takes hold, there emerges Vicdansaadet.

2. Myth of A Superpower

In one of my early works I once wrote, "America is a great country, built by great people". And it took me some time to look through the fallacy of this statement. I could still justify it by saying, it depends on the context - which would be technically true. But my dignity, my conscience, my morality - everything that is civilized in me, has been eating me alive for some time now over this one statement. Because if we throw away all technicality and look from a simple, everyday human perspective - nothing about the the birth of America is great - America is a terrorist nation, built by terrorists who invaded other people's land, stripped them of their homes, and built a spin-off of the ruthless British empire over their blood and bones. You think America's homeless problem is something new! It's not - America has been making people homeless ever since the pilgrims set foot in Plymouth Rock. The pilgrims were not pioneers, they were terrorists.

99 percent of the world's warzones are the legacy of white, western imperialism. Until

you get your head around this simple fact, your views, your opinion, your advocacy, all are worthless to the peace struggles of these "westsploited" nations.

In the modern age no other country has wrecked more nations than America. Like father, like son - first it was England, then it's its rebellious runaway child America. That's why China is such an enemy in the westwashed narrative of the world - because when one nation has somewhat maintained an autocratic control over the planet since the 1800s (under the banner of "Manifest Destiny"), it would never want that control be undermined by another budding power - particularly when that power is far superior in infrastructure. Sure, the state of China tries to influence every move of its people, that's the first unwritten rule in the handbook of "democracy" - but Uncle Sam has been manipulating the moves of every single state for over two hundred years. Now tell me, which state should you be more cautious of?

No country is free from human rights violation, but America's share in global transgressions is right at the very top. America is the top exporter of humanitarian crisis in the world, and as such, US is the least qualified nation to be the moral guardian on anything. You see, US is, not the Big Brother, but the Big Bully of the world.

ABHIJIT NASKAR

3. Redeeming Humanness

It doesn't matter whether you are white, colored or martian - denial never solves nothing. To treat a disease we must first acknowledge the disease. And what is the disease? Is it white people - is it whiteness? No - whiteness is not the disease, but white imperialism is. And how do you treat this disease? You gotta strip yourself of all the privileges of skin, and make yourself one with the world - you gotta denounce the privilege of your whiteness and embrace the responsibility of your humanness. Only then, shall there be peace in the world - only then, shall there be integration - only then, shall there be a civilized world to begin with.

So, this Fourth of July, instead of celebrating your Americanness, do something to redeem your humanness. Anybody can become a super power by exploiting and abusing others - that's not greatness, it's bestiality - but to grow super without trampling on anybody, that's greatness - better yet, to grow super together with everybody, that's absolute greatness.

But mark you, this ain't gonna be easy. The January 6 Insurrection is proof of how the animals would react when you try to right the wrongs that they have been clinging to for ages as heritage. Which means, if you wanna right the wrongs, you are bound to be called a traitor by your own people. Are you ready for that? Do you have the stomach for that? Do you have the backbone to stand up to those animals, knowing quite well that you will not live long enough to see the reform you struggle for?

If yes, only then there is hope - only then there is possibility - if yes, only then, perhaps one day, there will actually be an America of the humans, for the humans, by the humans.

And this applies not just to America, but to the whole world. Wherever you are, it is your existential duty as civilized human to stand up to animal behavior, whether they come from people in power or regular everyday civilians. Your society, your responsibility - correction - our society, our responsibility - it's that simple.

4. Unspoken Truths (The Sonnet)

Sonnet 1239

Unspoken Truths
(The Sonnet)

Democracy is people-approved dictatorship,
Military is people-approved genocide.
Atom bombs are people-approved armageddon,
In conscience-court all guilty of homicide.

There is no time left, for there never was time,
Time begins with the beginning of civilization.
And civilization is something we are yet to find,
Hence, there is no question of clock progression.

Nationalist chimps sell war in the name of security,
Stoneage civilians rush to bulk-buy graveyard plots.
Merchant of murder, you, yell about peacekeeping,
While you feast on nationalism like wet little cods!

When cavemen take pride in their national glory of death,
Sanctuary becomes asylum for the lunatic walking dead!

So the question is, how do we treat this condition. The answer is simple enough, but the practice not so much.

The answer is this.

Do not, I repeat - do not take anything and anyone as gospel – not even me.

I don't take law as gospel, I don't take goons as gospel, I don't take preachers, politicians, philosophers as gospel. If they misbehave in front of me, I will treat them as my own child, and teach them the lessons on civilized human behavior that their parents failed to teach.

Because of this attitude of mine, many accuse me of God complex. To which I say this - I don't think myself to be God - I am God - and I have only one mission - to flood the world with such Gods by the thousands, if not millions.

5. Ain't Hands But Hammer
(Reformer's Sonnet)

Sonnet 1240

Ain't Hands But Hammer
(Reformer's Sonnet)

Mine ain't hands but hammer -
to knock down walls of prejudice.
Mine ain't brain but bulldozer -
to crush all bigoted rubbish.

Brain is needed, brawn is needed,
More than all conscience is needed.
While the violent pretend to be gentle,
The gentle pretending violent, is needed.

Peace is not the absence of violence,
Peace is an act of controlled violence.
Controlled narcissism is a golden faculty,
To reform a society rooted in somnolence.

When all pretend gentle, I admit, I'm mental.
To the peace of intolerance, I'm damn detrimental.

Intolerance is born of insecurity, insecurity is born of ignorance. And since ignorance itself is a universal element of the human condition, intolerance as well, is a universal element of the condition. The next sonnet demonstrates.

34

6. Khalsa isn't Khalistan
(The Sonnet)

Sonnet 1241

Khalsa isn't Khalistan
(The Sonnet)

Khalsa means freedom from hate,
Khalistan means nationalizing hate.
Christ stands for love and compassion,
Chistian nationalism is Christ's death.

Sanatana Dharma is advaita sanskriti,
that is, a culture of nonsectarianism,
Hindutva means mindless saffronization.
Islam means working for peace and welfare,
Islamism is the ruin of synchronization.

Intolerance is a worldwide pandemic,
only terminologies vary culture to culture.
Vaccine for the mightiest swords of hate,
is the gentle glint of one heart, hatebuster.

Give me ten unarmed transformers of love and light,
I shall wipe out hate from its roots of fright.

7. Time to Defect (The Sonnet)

Sonnet 1242

Time to Defect
(The Sonnet)

It's time to defect, my friend -

from the side of passport to the side of heartport,
from the side of prison to the side of reason,
from the side of nationality to the side of sanity,
from the side of myopia to the side of motion,

from the side of crutches to the side of conscience,
from the side of coffins to the side of character,
from the side of bombs to the side of backbone,
from the side of barbwire to the side of brainwire,

from the side of flag to the side of fervor,
from the side of parasites to the side of paragons,
from the side of pacemakers to the side of peacemakers,
from the side of ideology to the side of illumination.

It's time to defect, my friend -
from the side of caves to the side of kind,
from the side of tribe to the side of life.

8. In Search of The Perfect Country

Yes, we gotta defect, not in the land outside, but in the land inside. We gotta make the journey within. We are all refugees inside our mind - a sentient being trying to escape its animal past towards a human future, and in doing so, we set the foundation for a civilized world.

So you see, it's not about changing your nationality.

If you want to move to a country where there is no human rights issue, you'd have to move to a different planet. No country is perfect, it doesn't have to be. As long as there are citizens who value progress over propaganda, and rights over ritual, there is hope for the country yet.

Remember one thing.

The perfect country doesn't exist, the perfect consciousness doesn't exist, the perfect cosmos doesn't exist. No hay país perfecto, no hay conciencia perfecta, no hay cosmos perfecto.

And in fact, this very insane obsession over perfection leaves the mind vulnerable to propaganda.

Now the question is, how do you distinguish propaganda from journalism?

Here's how.

In propaganda the media fixates on creating a negative narrative of certain nations and communities, whereas in journalism the good elements of a community get as much coverage as the bad elements, if not more.

Of course there are some extreme scenarios, such as Afghanistan, Russia and North Korea, but other than a select few utterly tyrannical states, every ordinary democratic country has its fair share of both good and bad.

Besides - the entire world is Afghanistan, you never felt it because either you are white or privileged.

9. Geopolitics 101

Wanna study geopolitics? First, take off your westwashed glasses - second, take off your westwashed shoes - third, scrub off your westwashed skin. In a world where the west has caused more humanitarian crises than Naskar has written books, you shall understand nothing till you decolonize your mind, no matter which hemisphere you are born in.

You see - there is no western world or eastern world, there is only human world - and till you get this simple fact, your opinion on life, liberty and justice is of no use.

But to get back to the matter at hand, all the governments of the world are incompetent in many things and competent in others. Incompetence is not the same as tyranny. Sure you must work to improve the quality of life in your nation - but at the same time, be grateful of the democracy you have, no matter how flawed it is - because in some parts of the world, your democracy would be deemed as a priceless blessing.

Fact of the matter is this.

The ordinary democratic governments of these ordinary democratic countries may have their usual autocratic tendencies like any system of government placed in power by the people to control national affairs, but none of them actually has neither the brains nor the backbone to achieve absolute autocratic control over the people. That is why, no matter how big and mighty the leaders of the democratic nations might appear to the world, at the back of their head they all have one universal fear - the fear of losing the next election.

Besides, it is far easier today to conquer the people with soft power than hard power.

The point is, you must be aware of a government's potential as well as its flaws, if you are to lift up the nation, as well as the world. But only an actual civilized human free from the grasp of puny political loyalty can do that. Only a mind free from puny political loyalty can perceive the potential of a state alongside its flaws, and put the potential to some good use, while also calling out the errors of the state, but not as signs of autocracy, but as plain, ordinary incompetence.

Remember this.

Allegiance destroys insight, insight destroys allegiance.

10. Takes Brains to be Dictator

The point is, it takes brains to be a dictator - mere dreaming of absolute control does nothing. For example, Donald Duck was the most incompetent president of American history, and even though he dreamed of absolute control over the American people, and thereafter the world, he did not have the brains for it. The only reason he survived his term in office was due to the heap-load of bigoted carcass - oops, I meant, caucus, of the republican party.

However, one thing did go wrong when that orange-haired orangutan came to power - all the bigots and fundamentalists of the world started dreaming once again to turn their own nations into a cradle of prehistoric hate, intolerance and fundamentalism.

And in this dream the most powerful weapon in their arsenal is culture. Know this - whenever a politician secretly dreams of autocracy, you'll hear them shout a lot about preserving the culture and tradition.

A civilized government is a nonsectarian government. Until you've learnt to walk on your own without the prosthetic of government, make sure the government you place in power is a nonsectarian one, or to be more politically accurate - make sure, it's a nonpartisan one.

I'll say to you plainly. Government is an outdated concept, and partisan government is downright prehistoric. I understand, if humankind is yet to invent the self-sustaining fabric of society that needs no government, but how can this so-called intelligent lifeform be so dumb as to still be slave to partisanism!

And what do you think will happen, when such a moronic species start to colonize other planets! I leave the answer to your better nonpartisan awareness - if you have any that is.

11. Space Exploration Ethics 101

If we can colonize Mars, we can heal the Earth. But that's not the point here. The point is, we gotta explore space just like we gotta explore anything unknown - but we must do so as humble scientists, not as steroid-pumped, illegitimate offspring of musky retards like Columbus.

We gotta explore space just like we explore the Arctic. Humankind has several outposts in the Arctic, dedicated solely to research - our endeavors into other planets oughta be exactly like that. Otherwise, what starts out as space exploration will soon turn into space imperialism, and will do to other planets what white terrorists have been doing to the indigenous people on earth for ages.

Therefore, focus on space exploration, not on space colonization. Let me put this into perspective. NASA, ISRO, CNSA, ESA, KARI, JAXA (and more) - these represent the real democratic aspirations of humankind's endeavors of curiosity into space, whereas SpaceX, Blue Origin, Virgin Galactic these are the new-age posterboys of space imperialism.

All I say is this, O Brave Explorers of Space - your mission is to explore the universe to facilitate human welfare, not to be some retarded billionaire's backboneless underwear. Beware, I repeat - space exploration doesn't turn into space imperialism!

12. Bursting Bubbles

On earth we are immigrants from Africa - out in space we'd be immigrants from Earth - in a different galaxy, we'd be immigrants from Milkyway. To put simply, in exploration of space, both external and internal, terms like immigrant and indigenous are meaningless. It's the heart that makes us indigenous or immigrant, not blood.

However, this grand vision of life can't be fathomed by bigoted, supremacist vermin still stuck in the stoneage. To them I say - if you are not indigenous, you are an immigrant - it's that simple. Try to remember that, next time you tell someone to go back to their country.

You see, animal habits are difficult to denounce - it takes a lot of courage and conscience. That's why colonial tendency is still so much rampant in psychologically backward countries like our US, and England. I mention these two in particular, because no other so-called modern country has caused more human rights violation across the world than these two - like father like son.

Heck, there is no star spangled banner, there is only blood stained banner - and there is no union jack, there is only union jerk!

You gotta acknowledge the disease first, to treat it. But instead if you celebrate the disease as a proud tradition of your social fabric, then I'm afraid, yours is not a society of humans, but a bush of baboons.

As a kid, like most kids in the third world, even I dreamed of moving to America. This was when Naskar was a nobody - but now that Naskar is a global icon, and has actually seen and understood the world, America is the last country I'd settle in, despite the fact that the majority of my readers are American.

Mark you, at this point, my geographical location makes no difference whatsoever - but if I ever do consider a new place of residence out of impulse alone, and not for work or love, America is no longer at the top of the list. Now I realize, why James Baldwin moved to France.

This is why true insight is so inconvenient - it destroys all your bubbles. And the sooner they burst, the sooner you'll be civilized. The

sooner they burst, the sooner you'll be human.
Now let's burst some more bubbles.

65

13. Humanitarian Nuclear Physics
(The Sonnet)

Sonnet 1243

Humanitarian Nuclear Physics
(The Sonnet)

One nuclear warhead contains 9 lbs of plutonium,
Which can electrify 2000 households for a year.
Yet you use that majestic power of atom as pawn,
In your stoneage geopolitical games of fear.

When monkeys crack the mystery of the atom,
Without developing any civilized purpose,
They go blind with the madness of power,
Atom bombs become newage arrows and spears.

Hypnotized by the mindless pursuit of "could",
Apes rarely ever stop to question if they should!
What good is such science without conscience,
What good is a scientist without a vision for good!

Either atom bombs will be obsolete as bow and arrow,
Or humankind will go extinct like dinosaurs tomorrow.

14. BnD (The Sonnet)

Sonnet 1244

BnD
(The Sonnet)

Same breasts that seduce a man,
Shelter the newborn as well.
A real man knows the difference,
Baboons behave eternally libidinal.

Real man looks a woman in the eyes,
They don't flutter in convenience,
While baboons are ever engrossed,
Between the twin-hills below neck.

There's a time and place for everything,
Well built character knows the difference.
If you're single and seeking, ask her out,
Real men don't think nasty, without consent.

Prime your penis only in bed,
that too to serve your partner.
Outside the bedroom backbone must reign,
while the "d" is kept as bodily sewer.

15. Activism and Hypocrisy

> Backbone has no gender,
> Backbone has no orientation.
> Backbone is plainly human,
> Backbone is brawn to ascension.

However things are never black and white,
Arrogance often masquerades as backbone.
Beware o human, of the clutches of animal,
That lurks within mind's corners unhoned.

One thing I hate most in this world, next to arrogance, is hypocrisy. Privileged teenagers hysterically yelling about climate action with no tangible contribution on their part - privileged celebrities flying in private jets, sipping fine wine, while barking about equal pay in a room full of other privileged celebrities - all these ain't activism, it's entitled lunacy. When you're struggling with your last ounce of strength to put food on the table, to keep a roof over your family, and still have some generosity left for your neighbors, that's the highest form of human rights struggle there is.

The world of justice looks very different depending on which side of disparity you belong to. For the everyday commoner, struggle for human rights is the natural way of life, whereas for privileged egomaniacs, activism is a publicity stunt. Send these entitled bunch of buffoons to labor in the streets of the developing parts of the world, and all their activism will fly out the window.

It's this simple. Before you start shouting about rights, equality and justice, have the decency and common sense to step out of the lap of privilege and luxury. Remember, there is no difference between a barking dog with golden platter and barking activist with a silver spoon. Struggle in the streets, struggle in the beaches, only then you shall know, what suits the humans, what suits the leeches.

16. Either Rich or Activist

I must also mention something crucial. My entire universe of work is a clarion call for acceptance. Hence, I say, even though I do not approve of luxury, I still stand willing to accept it - correction, I stand willing to tolerate it (for acceptance is too grand an act for something so petty as luxury).

What it means is that, just because they are rich, doesn't mean they are evil. My point is this - you can be rich and kind at the same time, but you cannot be rich and activist at the same time. Rich people cannot be activist, activists cannot be rich - no matter how the media designates them.

For example, there are many who swift-ly ease people's pain with their music and song-writing. They are rich and basically good people - but they don't go about pretending to be activist just to make a lot of noise. They do music, and they do it well, while being kind and gentle as much as possible. And that's all that really matters.

You don't need to be an activist to be good people, particularly when most activists of today are just attention-craving hypocrites. It's a sad and rather degrading state of affairs when populism gets rebranded as activism. As I said earlier, send these activists to struggle in developing parts of the world, and all their conviction will fade within a week.

17. I Don't Do Publicity

Is Abhijit Naskar famous? That's a question I've come across most often recently whenever I google myself - yes, I do google myself. So, I wonder - is Abhijit Naskar famous?

And here's what my mind comes up with.

There is a slight possibility, that you might not have heard of me. You know why? Because genius works in silence, mediocrity clings to noise. I write in silence, I publish in silence, I continue the struggle in silence - in silence and alone.

I don't do publicity, I never will. My entire body of works thrives despite the absolute absence of publicity. I don't have an industry to back me up - all I have is my dream - the dream of an undivided world.

Now enough with this nonsense of shallowness! Let's move on from the kingdom of animal shallowness to the realm of civilized substance.

The question is not whether you've heard of me, the real question is, have you found me in your heart yet?

Me as in, not the person, but the idea.

And what is the idea?

The idea of oneness - that's what my world is about - or better yet, that's what the civilized world is about - because the opposite facilitates shallowness - the opposite facilitates narrowness - the opposite facilitates hate, prejudice, death and division.

And this problem is not the problem of any specific nation or culture - it's the problem of the entire world - because it stems from the animal origin of humankind.

18. Beyond The Charade

Putting all philosophical idealism aside - in our intellectual naivety we cannot also turn a blind eye to the facts of history. Historically speaking, certain cultures were motivated by the savage dream of world domination, while others stood steadfast on their conviction of peaceful coexistence. And no matter which side of the spectrum you have descended from, no conscientious human can turn a blind eye to these atrocities of tradition.

Point is, bloodline doesn't make you a civilized human, your concern for human welfare does - universal human welfare.

Let me put it to you another way.

Naskar doesn't write for the white or colored, Naskar doesn't write for the believer or nonbeliever - Naskar doesn't write for the capitalist or socialist - Naskar only writes for the human - because Naskar is human - a whole human.

We are humans, and humanity is our supreme nationality - or better yet - humanity is our only nationality.

Do you understand what humanity means - what being human means?

The point is, the world is yet to understand humanity at its core, that's why they do make-believe with a load of linguistic jargon, like inclusion, diversity, justice and the entire lot.

First law of understanding - never submit to the entrapment of words - for every word has a definition, and every definition is constructed by a mentally sectarian and sick society. So, no matter how much you believe that you are getting the meaning just right - you are galaxies apart from any actual meaning - from any actual substance.

Learn to be a decent human being, and love, inclusion, justice, and all that, will pour out of your every footstep by law of nature, without all the intellectual charade - as well as spiritual charade.

19. Hate Can't Be Human

What's the first commandment - a fundamentalist preacher once yelled at me with utter condescension! I replied quite instinctively - love thy neighbor. He laughed in ridicule and said - if you had actually studied the bible, you'd know, the first commandment is, love thy God - love thy neighbor is the second.

I smiled and responded - and if you had paid any attention to my pal JC, you'd know - love comes first, nothing before that.

That's the problem with this world - too much doctrines, and too little awareness - too much indoctrination, and too little realization.

That's how love gets replace with hate, and reason with superstition.

I'll say it to you plainly.

Human can't hate, hate can't be human. Human can't be superstitious, superstition can't be human. The role of superstition is to sustain the animal, not the human. The role of aggression manifesting as hate is to sustain the animal, not the human.

Which means, it ultimately comes to a matter of choice. You got to choose - and upon your choice, fate of the world is predicated - fate of civilization is predicated.

Don't give in to rigidity - no matter what kind of a package it comes in - it may come in the form of religious identity, it may come in the form of cultural identity, it may come in the form of national identity - or any other sectarian identity. Let them come - you for one, stand strong - you for one, stand strong, never submitting to rigidity - never submitting to indoctrination - never submitting to the tradition of lifelessness.

20. Get Up, Get Out, Get Lost

The traditional form of sonnet contains four passages - first three with four lines each, and the last with two. However, often I find it more appropriate to fill all four passages with four lines each, and sometimes I even add one or two extra passages. This my friend, is called, evolution.

Remember, in life or in literature, forms are meant to serve the fervor, not the other way around - patterns are meant to serve the purpose, not the other way around. That's why, even though most times I make my sonnets rhyme, once in a while, the message is best expressed raw, without any rhyme. In short, don't be a slave to the pattern - use the pattern as it fits the purpose - and if necessary discard the pattern altogether.

And please, don't go about falling prey to more conspiracy theories surrounding the word "pattern" or "matrix".

Anyway, I'll put it to you plainly.

Rigidity ain't human, rigidity is animal - and the rigid can be a lot of things, but they ain't human - intellectual or not - religious or not - cultured or not.

From Karbala to Kurukshetra, from Jerusalem to Chanakkale, light of truth has never submitted to the howling audacity of divisive animality - then why should you? Remember, there is a karbala in each of you, there is a kurukshetra in each of you, there is a jerusalem and chanakkale in each of you. And till you accept defeat out of your own free will, not a force in the world can dampen the daring advances of love and reason.

So, get up - get out - and get lost!

Wanna lead the world? First learn about the world - get so lost in the struggles of each and every people of planet earth, that you forget where you came from altogether - get so lost in the struggles of the people of earth, that for the first time in life you start to breathe as a whole human being - get so lost, that for the first time you see the light of dawn not as a puny slave to puny borders, but as the civilized maker of a civilized world.

21. Intellect and Insight

Abandon all antiquated atrocities of superstitious stupidity, as well as newage intellectual puerility - only then you shall develop the wholesome insight into what's right and what's wrong - or better yet - what's kind, what's not.

Intellect is a part of insight, not the whole of it - what's more important - intellect is not the cause of insight. Insight is the cause of everything civilized, not the other way around.

Intellect without insight is incapable of constructing a civilized world - it may create a world externally advanced for sure, but internally, such world would be just as backward and barbarian as a world without intellect. Intellect is supposed to enhance our humanity, not undermine it.

The same holds true for faith. Faith tethered solely to books and not the heart, inadvertently becomes a breeding ground of superstition, bigotry and prejudice. Such faith is no more civilized than those of the jungle when our ancestors used to worship the elements of nature.

Here's the thing.

We gotta move from worship of savages roots out of fear and insecurity, to the worship of civilized roots out of a sense of service. And in service who do we worship - we worship ourselves - or to be particular, we worship the forgotten and the discriminated of society. And how do we worship these people who are but reflections of ourselves - we worship them by lifting them up - we worship them by elevating their living conditions.

In short, worship of the civilized is an act of service, where we are the worshipper, and our deity, the discriminated. Call it humanism, humanitarian, socialism, or by any other fancy, rotten intellectual title - to me, it's just an act of life. Worship is an act of service, and service is an act of life.

22. My Dream is One World Family

Where there is life, there is love - where there is life, there is justice - where there is life, there is inclusion - where there is life, there is oneness. In short - life is love - life is justice - life is inclusion - life is oneness.

It's this simple, then why do you complicate it so much - some with scriptures, others with intellectualism.

Let me put it another way for perspective.

Intellect is my servant, belief is my servant - I use them as I see fit. I as in - a whole human mind - untainted by the nonsense of ism - untainted by any sort of divisionism whatsoever.

But mark you, if you confuse all this with the notion of one world government - then I'm afraid, you've understood not a word of my life.

My dream is one world family, not one world government – my dream is a world where civilians bear the responsibility for the affairs of their society according to their capacity and expertise, not some halfwit political overlords.

The mission is to build a nonpartisan world, not to delegate all social responsibilities from countless little puny political nitwits to one giant global git.

And if you think, it's too much of a stretch, think again. The world is already run by such dedicated civilians, but alas, they don't get any credit or recognition for it. They are the doctors, teachers, scientists, janitors, construction workers, waitresses, bus drivers, train drivers, pilots and many more - these everyday, ordinary people do all the job, while populist politicians siphon all the credit.

Now please, don't go about making childish remarks like, how can I say all politicians are evil! Of course they are not - quite like winning the lottery, among the heap of cowdung, few may turn out to be good people. But my problem is not with politicians, my problem is with the very paradigm that declares a bunch of know-nothing idiots as the controller of people's lives simply based on their popularity.

It's like seeking medical advice from influencers because they have a huge social media following. O, wait - some of you actually do seek medical advice from influencers because they have a huge social media following. If that's your idea of a democratic society, you are better off living under the dictatorship of savages like Hitler or the British Monarch.

If any of this makes any sense, then there is hope yet - otherwise, dump me in the bin and get on with your fifty shades of grey.

23. End of Mindlessness

Keep struggling, o brave soldier - keep struggling till politicians become an extinct species and politics an extinct profession. The mission is, not to replace old world mindlessness with new world mindlessness, but to put an end to all forms of brainless authoritarianism selected randomly on the basis of charisma and popularity by hysterical whim.

The mission, I repeat, is to build a one world family, not one world government. Till the very word "government" is nowhere to be found but in books on ancient tribal rituals, keep on struggling, O Sapiens Impossible!

Only you can change the world, not you the person, but you the idea. It's never about the person - it's about the fervor within the person. When the fervor is strongly grounded in assimilation, no tradition of ignorance, bigotry and prejudice can deter the person from their existential core of conscience and compassion.

You don't need to run for office to change the world. In fact, it's better if you don't.

However, if you think you can do the most by running for office, then by all means do so (I hold my dream dear, but more than that, I hold nonrigidity dear).

The point is this, the path and the person must become one - only then you shall cause some lasting impact.

24. Either Right or Human

Since we did mention the matter of running for office, let's clear some long-standing air. You may lean leftwards or not - best would be to run as an independent, without any party affiliation - but whatever you do, do not lean rightwards - unless of course you are reading me in a distant future where the right has successfully mended its bigoted tendencies, and struggles for inclusion and equality like any other civilized force of society.

As of today, that's not the case. Sure, the left has its own issues, but they are not as savage and prehistoric as those of the right. Hence, I may not make much mention of the left, because I don't feel the need for it, but more and more I'm finding it difficult to stay neutral.

Let me put it this way.

More your understand the universe, harder it is to believe in a supreme, omniscient entity concerned with the welfare of a puny lifeform on a tiny blue dot - likewise, more you realize the endemic inequalities of society, harder it is to stay neutral.

You cannot understand equality, till you realize inequality. You cannot understand reason, till you realize superstition. You cannot understand justice, till you realize injustice. So, first and foremost, you gotta realize what's wrong with this world - then you shall have the necessary insight to move ahead with a just course of treatment.

As things are today, either you are right or human - it's that simple.

25. Psychoanalysis of The Right

When you get down to it - the phrase "right wing" is not the trouble, the real trouble is what it represents. And what does it represent? Think about what it represents at the present time, and you'd realize, why neutrality itself is inhuman in this matter.

It represents discrimination, prejudice, xenophobia, systemic racism, police brutality, religious fundamentalism, abortion ban, homophobia, climate denial and what not! Think of a primitive habit, and chances are, you'll find the right to be an ardent admirer of that habit as their proud tradition.

Put simply, you don't need to be left wing to recognize the inhumanities of the right, just like you don't need to be a woman to recognize the atrocities of patriarchy.

And that's the disease we gotta treat.

We gotta treat every last trace of prejudice, discrimination, intolerance, brutality and conspiracy theory, till we have nothing more significant to struggle for, than who gets to eat the last donut.

But again, as I said earlier, the mission is to build a one world family, not one world government. Therefore, by demolishing all bigotry and superstition, it's not a left wing world we gotta build - what we gotta build is a human world. Because, believe you me, too much obsession with one-sided wings eventually ends up in mental castration. Focus on the wind, not on the wings.

26. Be Human, Not Left

Struggle to put an end to bigotry and superstition wherever you find them - not because you are left or anything, but because you are human - just like, we gotta be kind in life, not because we are charitable, but because we are human.

My dream is to deliver the world with two whole wings, not left and right wings, but two human wings.

Only with two human wings true flight of the mind is possible - only with two nonsectarian wings true flight of humankind is possible - only with two nondualistic wings true flight of civilization is possible.

Point is, we gotta have a sense of practicality towards the present while fostering a grand vision of the future, even if that vision appears to be absurd by measures of all the cold, mechanical calculations of a somnolent society.

We gotta do what betters today, but at the same time, we gotta make arrangements for even a better tomorrow. Idealism won't do.

Make no compromise on your vision, but you must adjust your initiatives according to the requirements of the ages. By requirements, I don't mean the demands that society makes of you - rather, I am asking you to chart your course of action befitting the conditions of the present, and not solely to flatter a mythical future.

You gotta mould the future out of the present, not separate from it. The present is the clay, conscience is the craftsman.

So, what are you waiting for?

Go ahead and mould it.

Mould it with your every word,
mould it with your every breath,
mould it with your every thought,
mould it with your footsteps.

27. Time is Illusion (The Sonnet)

Sonnet 1245

Time is Illusion
(The Sonnet)

Time is a necessary illusion,
forged from the fabric of memory,
meant for adding coherence to life,
so that you're mindful of your duty.

Body cannot survive in the vacuum of space,
Mind cannot survive in the vacuum of time.
Brain cannot survive in the vacuum of skull,
So it floats about in the fluid of spine.

Memory makes the past, memory makes future,
Memory is the bedrock of the time psyche.
Physical time is irrelevant to the mind,
Mind creates its own domain of temporality.

Time is a myth, that aids us survive.
Master the myth, o divine maker -
Time and tide are born inside!

128

28. Sonnet of Myths

Sonnet 1246

Sonnet of Myths

Myths are healthy for creativity,
If you can tell myths from reality.
Imagination is almost a superpower,
If you can wield it without conspiracy.

Imagination is a boon to creativity,
Same time it can facilitate conspiracy.
Imagination out of touch with common sense,
Ends up being an ingredient of animality.

Imagination can bring light or it can
worsen society's darkness predominant.
It all depends on how you wield it,
as a force for expansion or contraction!

All through history myths have peddled contraction,
They are used to cripple the mind's flightful spirit.
Enough I say, with the hegemony of dead habit,
Crashing all convention of contraction, off you go, lift!

29. Not Left, But Human
(The Sonnet)

Sonnet 1247

Not Left, But Human
(The Sonnet)

Inclusion is not left, inclusion is human.
Reason is not left, reason is human.
Equality is not left, equality is human.
Choice is not left, choice is but human.

Science is not left, science is but human.
Justice is not left, justice is but human.
Secularism is not left, secularism is human,
Acceptance is not left, acceptance is human.

Interfaith is not left, interfaith is human.
Integration is not left, integration is human.
Harmony is not left, harmony is but human.
Oneness is not left, oneness is but human.

Oneness is the path, oneness makes civilization.
To be kind is not left – to be kind is to be human.

30. One World Family
(The Sonnet)

Sonnet 1248

One World Family
(The Sonnet)

My dream is, one world family,
not one world government.
My vision calls for a human world,
beyond the battle of right and left.

Trading Nato for Brics ain't advancement,
Swapping Sam with Soviet isn't progress.
If your mistrust of one colonizer
makes you build alliance with another,
it's not change but recurring regress.

Change is only change when
inhumanity is rejected altogether.
If inhumanity merely changes carrier,
it's not change but diplomatic disaster.

Alliance after alliance, cult after cult,
Politics over people will destroy the world.
All alliance stem from interest not integration,
Such geopolitical diplomacy will be our castration.

140

31. North, South, East, West
(The Sonnet)

Sonnet 1249

North, South, East, West
(The Sonnet)

North, South, East, West,
Get rid of this nonsense.
Spend some time at the ISS,
You shall foster unified sense.

Unified sense is civilized sense,
All other sense is but animal.
No matter how advanced you think you are,
Till you realize love you're animal.

Fearless, you reach out
to bring smiles in lives gone cheerless.
Stateless, you cross borders
to equalize the discriminated.

North, South, East, West,
Abandon all primitive divide.
Your culture is my culture,
Together alone shall we thrive!

32. World Integration Day
(9th October Sonnet)

Sonnet 1250

World Integration Day
(9th October Sonnet)

When I am gone,

Celebrate not October 9th,
as the day Naskar was born.
Celebrate it if you so desire,
as the World Day of Integration.

Tie a bracelet of assimilation,
amongst buddies across culture.
Pledge to have each other's back,
even if deemed tradition's traitor.

Mark you, one day is not enough,
to live as an integration advocate.
But the journey of a million miles,
must begin with one bold step.

Live each day of your life,
as proof of love and oneness.
Cause inclusion defying prejudice,
You are the cure for divisiveness.

149

33. Sonnet 1251

Sonnet 1251

You are the captain,
You are the coxswain,
You are the world's oar!
You are the catalyst,
You are the analyst,
You are the tether to shore!

You are the time, you are the tide.
You are the vessel of love and light!
You are the space, you are the ship.
You are in a brain, light-years of sight!

You are plutonium, you are uranium,
You are the alchemist of destiny!
Fire to the cold, water to the thirsty,
You are the answer to inhumanity.

You are unity, you are trinity,
You are the end of all animosity!
You are able, always accountable,
You are the measure of living sanity!

153

33. Sonnet 1252

Sonnet 1252

This earth is my home,
This earth is my dream.
Born in this earth's soil,
To no sect I'll ever give in.

Born of soil, die in soil -
Breathe in soil, break in soil.
Better break to a million pieces,
Than submit to sectarian turmoil.

Know your roots, know your nature,
Step out of your tribal stretcher.
You got a mind full of atomic light,
Where did you lose your himalayan vigor!

Vigor awake, figure awake!
Vanguard you are, vanguard you stand!
Atoms awake, armor awake!
Amidst the powercut you are powerbank.

157

34. Here on Earth

All said and done, in our headstrong struggle for inclusion, we mustn't also underestimate everything we have achieved so far as a species. As a matter of fact, we've come a long way since our tribal days of division and discrimination. Let me show you how. World's most beloved poet, Mevlana Rumi, was a muslim - world's icon of civil rights, MLK, was a black person - world's greatest inspiration of science, Albert Einstein, was a German Jew - and most recently, as of 2023, PM of UK and VP of US, both are of Indian origin.

So don't tell me, we've achieved nothing - don't tell me, there is no hope for integration! Integration is happening all over the world, despite the ancient impediments of intolerance and hate. Therefore, the question is not whether integration is possible - real question is, are you a part of that integration, or aren't you! Our home is planet earth - and here on earth, we all cry the same pain, smile the same joy, and live the same love.

BIBLIOGRAPHY

Archer M., (2000), Being Human: The Problem of Agency. Cambridge University Press.

Adolphs R (2003) Cognitive neuroscience of human social behaviour. Nature Rev Neurosci 4: 165–178.

Adolphs R, Tranel D, Damasio AR (2003) Dissociable neural systems for recognizing emotions. Brain Cogn 52: 61–69.

Andresen, Jensine, and Robert Forman, eds. Cognitive Models and Spiritual Maps. Bowling Green, Ohio: Imprint Academic, 2000.

Bernstein R.J., (1971), Praxis and Action: Contemporary Philosophies of Human Activity. Philadelphia: University of Pennsylvania Press.

Bernstein R.J., (1976), The Restructuring Social and Political Thought.

Bogen, J.E.(1995a), 'On the neurophysiology of consciousness: Part I. An overview', Consciousness and Cognition, 4.

Bogen, J.E. (1995b), 'On the neurophysiology of consciousness: Part II. Constraining the semantic problem', Consciousness and Cognition, 4.

Bremner, J. D., R. Soufer, et al. (2001). "Gender differences in cognitive and neural correlates of remembrance of emotional words." Psychopharmacol Bull 35 (3).

Brothers, L. (2002). The social brain: A project for integrating primate behavior and neurophysiology in a new domain. In J. T. Cacioppo et al. (Eds.), Foundations in neuroscience. Cambridge, MA: MIT Press.

Buss, D. D. (2003). Evolutionary Psychology: The New Science of Mind, 2nd ed. New York: Allyn & Bacon.

Buss, D. M. (1989). "Conflict between the sexes: Strategic interference and the evocation of anger and upset." J Pers Soc Psychol 56 (5).

Buss, D. M. (1995). "Psychological sex differences. Origins through sexual selection." Am Psychol 50 (3).

Buss, D. M., and D. P. Schmitt (1993). "Sexual strategies theory: An evolutionary perspective on human mating." Psychol Rev 100 (2).

Chomsky Noam, (2016) Who Rules the World?

Churchland, P.S. (1986), Neurophilosophy (Cambridge, MA: The MIT Press).

Churchland, P.S. & Ramachandran, V.S. (1993), 'Filling in: Why Dennett is wrong', in Dennett and His Critics:

Demystifying Mind, ed. B. Dahlbom (Oxford: Blackwell Scientific Press).

Churchland, P.S., Ramachandran, V.S. & Sejnowski, T.J. (1994), 'A critique of pure vision', in Large- scale Neuronal Theories of the Brain, ed. C. Koch & J.L. Davis (Cambridge, MA: The MIT Press).

Crick, F. (1994), The Astonishing Hypothesis: The Scientific Search for the Soul (New York: Simon and Schuster).

Crick, F. (1996), 'Visual perception: rivalry and consciousness', Nature, 379.

Crick, F. & Koch, C. (1992), 'The problem of consciousness', Scientific American, 267.

d'Aquili, Eugene. "Senses of Reality in Science and Religion." Zygon 17, no 4 (1982)

d'Aquili, Eugene. "The Biopsychological Determinants of Religious Ritual Behavior." Zygon 10, no. 1 (1975)

d'Aquili, Eugene. "The Myth-Ritual Complex: A Biogenetic Structural Analysis." Zygon 18, no. 3 (1983)

d'Aquili, Eugene, and Andrew Newberg. The Mystical Mind: Probing the Biology of Religious Experience. Minneapolis: Fortress Press, 1999.

Damasio, A. (1994) Descartes' Error: Emotion, Reason and the Human Brain. New York, Putnams.

Damasio, A. (1999) The Feeling of What Happens: Body, Emotion and the Making of Consciousness. London, Heinemann.

Darwin, C. (1859) On the Origin of Species by Means of Natural Selection. London, Murray.

Darwin, C. (1871) The Descent of Man and Selection in Relation to Sex. London, John Murray.

Dawkins, R. (1976) The Selfish Gene. Oxford, Oxford University Press; a new edition, with additional material, was published in 1989.

Dewhurst, Kenneth, and A. W. Beard. "Sudden Religious Conversions in Temporal Lobe Epilepsy." British Journal of Psychiatry 117 (1970)

Dewhurst K, Beard AW. Sudden religious conversions in temporal lobe epilepsy. 1970 Epilepsy Behav 2003

Devinsky O, Lai G. Spirituality and religion in epilepsy. Epilepsy Behav 2008.

E. Horvitz, "One Hundred Year Study on Artificial Intelligence: Reflections and Framing," ed: Stanford University, 2014.

Eckhart Meister, Selected Writings

Farah, M.J. (1989), 'The neural basis of mental imagery', Trends in Neurosciences, 10.

Freud, S. "Selected papers on hysteria and other psychoneuroses" Journal of Nervous and Mental Disease 1909.

Freud, S. "The Origin and Development of Psychoanalysis", 1910

Freud, S. "Psychopathology of everyday life", 1914

Freud, S. "Beyond the Pleasure Principle", 1920

Frith, C.D. & Dolan, R.J. (1997), 'Abnormal beliefs: Delusions and memory', Paper presented at the May, 1997, Harvard Conference on Memory and Belief.

Gay, Volney, ed. Neuroscience and Religion. Plymouth, UK: Lexington Books, 2009.

Gazzaniga, M. S. (1985). The social brain. New York: Basic Books.

Gazzaniga, M.S. (1993), 'Brain mechanisms and conscious experience', Ciba Foundation Symposium, 174.

Geschwind N. "Behavioural changes in temporal lobe epilepsy". Psychol Med. 1979.

Gellhorn, E., Kiely, W.F. "Mystical states of consciousness: neurophysiological and clinical aspects." J Nerv Ment Dis. 1972;154:399-405.

Gilbert SL, Dobyns WB, Lahn BT (2005) Genetic links between brain development and brain evolution. Nat Rev Genet 6.

Gray JA. The Psychology of Fear and Stress. 2nd ed. New York, NY: Cambridge University Press; 1988.

Gloor, P. (1992), 'Amygdala and temporal lobe epilepsy', in The Amygdala: Neurobiological Aspects of Emotion, Memory and Mental

Dysfunction, ed J.P. Aggleton (New York: Wiley-Liss).

Gross CG, Rocha-Miranda CE, Bender DB (1972) Visual properties of neurons in the inferotemporal cortex of the macaque. J Neurophysiol 35: 96–111.

Guevara Che, The Motorcycle Diaries, 1992

Hardy, G. H. (1940). Ramanujan. Cambridge: Cambridge University Press.

Hall, Daniel, Keith Meador, and Harold Koenig. "Measuring Religiousness in Health Research: Review and Critique." Journal of Religion and Health 47, no. 2 (2008)

Harris, Sam, Jonas Kaplan, Ashley Curiel, Susan Bookheimer, Marco Iacoboni, and Mark Cohen. "The Neural Correlates of Religious and Nonreligious Belief." PLoS One 4, no. 10 (October 1, 2009)

Halgren, E. (1992), 'Emotional neurophysiology of the amygdala within the context of human cognition', in The Amygdala: Neurobiological Aspects of Emotion, Memory and Mental Dysfunction, ed J.P. Aggleton (New York: Wiley-Liss).

Halligan PW, Fink GR, Marshal JC, Vallar G. 2003. Spatial cognition: evidence from visual neglect. Trends Cogn Sci.

Handbook of Emotions, Edited by Michael Lewis, Jeannette M. Haviland-Jones, and Lisa Feldman Barrett, The Guilford Press; 3rd edition (2010).

Hameroff, S.R. and Penrose, R. (1996) Conscious events as orchestrated space-time selections. Journal of Consciousness Studies 3(1), 36-53; also reprinted in J. Shear (ed.) (1997) Explaining Consciousness-The Hard Problem. Cambridge, MA, MIT Press, 177-95.

Harding, D.E. (1961) On Having no Head: Zen and the Re-Discovery of the Obvious. London, Buddhist Society.

Hardy, A. (1979) The Spiritual Nature of Man: A Study of Contemporary Religious Experience. Oxford, Clarendon Press.

Harre, R. and Gillett, G. (1994) The Discursive Mind. Thousand Oaks, CA, Sage.

Haugeland, J. (ed.) (1997) Mind Design II: Philosophy, Psychology, Artificial Intelligence. Cambridge, MA, MIT Press.

Hauser, M.D. (2000) Wild Minds: What Animals Really Think. New York, Henry Holt and Co.; London, Penguin.

Hilgard, E.R. (1986) Divided Consciousness: Multiple Controls in Human Thought and Action. New York, Wiley.

Hilton, E.N., Lundberg, T.R. Transgender Women in the Female Category of Sport: Perspectives on Testosterone Suppression and Performance Advantage. Sports Med 51, 199–214 (2021).

Hitler, Adolf. Mein Kampf, 1925

Hodgson, R. (1891) A case of double consciousness. Proceedings of the Society for Psychical Research 7, 221-58.

Hofstadter, D.R. and Dennett, D.C. (eds) (1981) The Mind's I: Fantasies and Reflections on Self and Soul. London, Penguin.

Holland, J. (ed.) (2001) Ecstasy: The Complete Guide: A Comprehensive Look at the Risks and Benefits of MDMA. Rochester, VT, Park Street Press.

Holmes, D.S. (1987) The influence of meditation versus rest on physiological arousal. In M. West (ed.)

The Psychology of Meditation. Oxford, Clarendon Press, 81-103.

Holmstrom, David. 1992, Christian Science Monitor

Holloway RL (1996) Evolution of the human brain. In: Lock A, Peters CR (eds) Handbook of human symbolic evolution. Oxford University Press, Oxford

Jeannerod M (1988) The neural and behavioural organization of goal-directed movements. Clarendon Press, Oxford.

Johnson-Frey SH, Maloof FR, Newman-Norlund R, Farrer C, Inati S, Grafton ST (2003) Actions or hand-objects interactions? Human inferior frontal cortex and action observation. Neuron 39: 1053–1058.

Jackson, F. (1982) Epiphenomenal qualia. Philosophical Quarterly 32, 127-36.

James, W. (1890) The Principles of Psychology (2 volumes). London, Macmillan.

James, W. (1902) The Varieties of Religious Experience: A Study in Human Nature. New York and London, Longmans, Green and Co.

Jansen, K. (2001) Ketamine: Dreams and Realities. Sarasota, FL, Multidisciplinary Association for Psychedelic Studies.

Jay, M. (ed.) (1999) Artificial Paradises: A Drugs Reader. London, Penguin.

Jaynes, J. (1976) The Origin of Consciousness in the Breakdown of the Bicameral Mind. New York, Houghton Mifflin.

Kandel, E. R. In Search of Memory: The Emergence of a New Science of Mind, W. W. Norton & Company (2007).

Kandel E. R. Schwartz JH, Jessel TM. Principles of neural sciences. New York; McGraw Hill, 2000.

Kanwisher, N. (2001) Neural events and perceptual awareness. Cognition 79, 89-113; also reprinted inS. Dehaene (ed.) The Cognitive Neuroscience of Consciousness. Cambridge, MA, MIT Press, 89-113.

Kihlstrom, J.F. (1996) Perception without awareness of what is perceived, learning without awareness of what is learned. In M. Velmans (ed.) The Science of Consciousness. London, Routledge, 23-46.

Kosslyn, S.M. (1980) Image and Mind. Cambridge, MA, Harvard University Press.

Kosslyn, S.M. (1988) Aspects of a cognitive neuroscience of mental imagery. Science 240, 1621-6.

Kjaer, Troels, Camilla Bertelsen, Paola Piccini, David Brooks, Jorgen Alving, and Hans Lou. "Increased Dopamine Tone during Meditation- Induced Change of Consciousness." Cognitive Brain Research 13, no. 2 (April 2002)

Kölmel HW. 1985. Complex visual hallucinations in the hemianopic field. J Neurol Neurosurg Psychiatry.

Koenig, Harold. "Research on Religion, Spirituality, and Mental Health: A Review." Canadian Journal of Psychiatry 54, no. 5 (May 2009)

Koenig, Harold, ed. Handbook of Religion and Mental Health. San Diego, CA: Academic Press, 1998

Kraepelin E. Psychiatry: A Textbook for Students and Physicians. New York, NY: Science History Publications; 1990.

Lauglin, Charles, John McManus, and Eugene d'Aquili. Brain, Symbol, and Experience. 2nd ed. New York: Columbia University Press, 1992

Lakoff, G. and M. Johnson (1999). Philosophy in the flesh. Basic Books: New York.

LeDoux, J. E. (1996). The emotional brain. New York: Simon & Schuster.

LeDoux, J.E. (1992), 'Emotion and the amygdala', in The Amygdala: Neurobiological Aspects of Emo- tion, Memory and Mental Dysfunction, ed J.P. Aggleton (New York: Wiley-Liss).

Levin, D.T. and Simons, D.J. (1997) Failure to detect changes to attended objects in motion pictures. Psychonomic Bulletin and Review 4, 501-6.

Levine,J. (1983) Materialism and qualia: the explanatory gap. Pacific Philosophical Quarterly 64, 354-61.

Levine,J. (2001) Purple Haze: The Puzzle of Consciousness. New York, Oxford University Press. Levine, S. (1979) A Gradual Awakening. New York, Doubleday.

Levinson, B.W. (1965) States of awareness during general anaesthesia. British Journal of Anaesthesia 37, 544-6.

Lewicki, P., Czyzewska, M. and Hoffman, H. (1987) Unconscious acquisition of complex procedural knowledge. Journal of Experimental Psychology: Learning, Memory and Cognition 13, 523-30.

Naskar, Abhijit. "What is Mind?", 2016

Naskar, Abhijit. "Love, God & Neurons: Memoir of A Scientist who found himself by getting lost", 2016

Naskar, Abhijit. "Principia Humanitas", 2017

Naskar, Abhijit. "We Are All Black: A Treatise on Racism", 2017

Naskar, Abhijit. "Either Civilized or Phobic: A Treatise on Homosexuality", 2017

Naskar, Abhijit. "Build Bridges not Walls: In the name of Americana", 2018

Naskar, Abhijit. "Citizens of Peace: Beyond the Savagery of Sovereignty", 2019

Naskar, Abhijit. "The Constitution of The United Peoples of Earth", 2019

Naskar, Abhijit. "Mission Reality", 2019

Naskar, Abhijit. "Good Scientist: When Science and Service Combine", 2020

Newberg, Andrew, and Jeremy Iversen. "The Neural Basis of the Complex Mental Task of Meditation: Neurotransmitter and Neurochemical Considerations." Medical Hypotheses 61, no. 2 (2003).

Newberg, Andrew. "How God Changes Your Brain: An Introduction to Jewish Neurotheology", CCAR

Journal: The Reform Jewish Quarterly, Winter 2016.

Newberg, Andrew, and Stephanie Newberg. "A Neuropsychological Perspective on Spiritual Development." In Handbook of Spiritual Development in Childhood and Adolescence, edited by Eugene Roehlkepartain, Pamela King, Linda Wagener, and Peter Benson. London: Sage Publications, Inc., 2005

Newberg, Andrew. "The Neurotheology Link An Intersection Between Spirituality and Health", Alternative and Complimentary Therapies, Vol 21 No 1, February 2015.

Newberg, Andrew, Nancy Wintering, Dharma Khalsa, Hannah Roggenkamp, and Mark Waldman. "Meditation Effects on Cognitive Function and Cerebral Blood Flow in Subjects with Memory Loss: A Preliminary Study." Journal of Alzheimer's Disease 20, no. 2 (2010)

Nash, M. (1995), 'Glimpses of the mind', Time.

Nesse RM. Proximate and evolutionary studies of anxiety, stress and depression: synergy at the interface. Neurosci Biobehav Rev. 1999;23:895-903.

Nicolelis, Miguel. (2011) "Beyond Boundaries: The New Neuroscience of Connecting Brains with Machines---and How It Will Change Our Lives", Times Books

O'Hara, K. and Scutt, T. (1996) There is no hard problem of consciousness. Journal of Consciousness Studies 3(4), 290-302, reprinted in J. Shear (ed.) (1997) Explaining Consciousness. Cambridge, MA, MIT Press, 69-82.

O'Regan, J.K. and Noe, A. (2001) A sensorimotor account of vision and visual consciousness. Behavioral and Brain Sciences 24(5), 883-917.

Ornstein, R.E. (1977) The Psychology of Consciousness (2nd edn). New York, Harcourt.

Ornstein, R.E. (1986) The Psychology of Consciousness (3rd edn). New York, Pehguin.

Ornstein, R.E. (1992) The Evolution of Consciousness. New York, Touchstone.

Penfield W, Faulk ME (1955) The insula: further observations on its function. Brain 78: 445– 470.

Penrose, R. (1994), Shadows of the Mind (Oxford: Oxford University Press).

Penrose, R. (1989), The Emperor's New Mind: Concerning Computers, Minds and The Laws of Physics (Oxford: Oxford University Press).

Persinger, "'I would kill in God's name' role of sex, weekly church attendance, report of a religious experience and limbic lability" Perceptual and Motor Skills 1997.

Persinger "Experimental simulation of the God experience" Neurotheology 2003.

Persinger, Corradini, Clement, Keaney, et al "Neurotheology and its convergence with neuroquantology" NeuroQuantology 2010.

Persinger. "The neuropsychiatry of paranormal experiences". J Neuropsychiatry Clin Neurosci 2001.

Persinger. "Neuropsychological bases of god beliefs", New York: Praeger, 1987

Persinger. "Temporal lobe epileptic signs and correlative behaviors displayed by normal populations", Journal of General Psychology, 1986

Perry BD, Pollard R. Homeostasis, stress, trauma, and adaptation. A neurodevelopmental view of childhood trauma. Child Adolesc Psychiatr Clin N Am. 1998;7:33.

Ramachandran VS. Behavioral and magnetoencephalographic correlates of plasticity in the adult human brain. Proc Natl Acad Sci USA 1993; 90: 10413–20.

Ramachandran VS. Plasticity and functional recovery in neurology. Clin Med 2005; 5: 368–73.

Rock I, Victor J. Vision and touch: an experimentally created conflict between the two senses. Science 1964; 143: 594–6.

Roberts, TA; Smalley, J; Ahrendt, D (December 2020). "Effect of gender affirming hormones on athletic performance in transwomen and transmen: implications for sporting organisations and legislators". British Journal of Sports Medicine. 55 (11): 577–583

Royet JP, Plailly J, Delon-Martin C, Kareken DA, Segebarth C (2003) fMRI of emotional responses to odors: influence of hedonic valence and judgment, handedness, and gender. Neuroimage 20: 713–728.

Rozin R Haidt J and McCauley CR (2000) Disgust. In: Lewis M, Haviland-Jones JM (eds) Handbook of Emotion. 2nd Edition. Guilford Press, New York, pp 637–653.

Saxe R, Carey S, Kanwisher N (2004) Understanding other minds: linking developmental psychology and functional neuroimaging. Annu Rev Psychol 55: 87–124.

S. J. Russell and P. Norvig, Artificial intelligence: a modern approach (3rd edition): Prentice Hall, 2009.

Singer T, Seymour B, O'Doherty J, Kaube H, Dolan RJ, Frith CD (2004) Empathy for pain involves the affective but not the sensory components of pain. Science 303: 1157–1162.

Smith A (1759) The theory of moral sentiments (ed. 1976). Clarendon Press, Oxford.

Schilling, Vincent. 2017, indian country today

Stein, Stephen K. 2017, The Sea in World History: Exploration, Travel, and Trade

Tesla N. "My Inventions", 1919

T. R. Society, "Machine learning: the power and promise of computers that learn by example," ed. The Royal Society, 2017.

Tomasello M, Call J (1997) Primate cognition. Oxford University Press, Oxford

191

193

www.ingramcontent.com/pod-product-compliance
Lightning Source LLC
Chambersburg PA
CBHW051257250726
48656CB00004B/1332